ANIMALS AT RISK
Sea Turtles in Danger

BY MICHAEL PORTMAN

Gareth Stevens
Publishing

Please visit our website, www.garethstevens.com. For a free color catalog of all our high-quality books, call toll free 1-800-542-2595 or fax 1-877-542-2596.

Library of Congress Cataloging-in-Publication Data

Portman, Michael, 1976-
Sea turtles in danger / Michael Portman.
     p. cm. — (Animals at risk)
Includes index.
ISBN 978-1-4339-5804-5 (pbk.)
ISBN 978-1-4339-5805-2 (6-pack)
ISBN 978-1-4339-5802-1 (library binding)
1. Sea turtles—Juvenile literature. 2. Sea turtles—Conservation—Juvenile literature. I. Title.
QL666.C536P67 2012
597.92'8—dc22

                                    2011001656

First Edition

Published in 2012 by
Gareth Stevens Publishing
111 East 14th Street, Suite 349
New York, NY 10003

Designer: Haley W. Harasymiw
Editor: Therese M. Shea

Photo credits: Cover, pp. 1, 4, 5, 11, 17, 19, 20 Shutterstock.com; p. 7 DEA/P. Jaccod/De Agostini/Getty Images; p. 9 Demetrio Carrasco/Dorling Kindersley/Getty Images; p. 13 T. O'Keefe/Photolink/Getty Images; p. 15 Norbert Wu/ Science Fiction Jewels/Getty Images.

Printed in the United States of America

CPSIA compliance information: Batch #CS11GS: For further information contact Gareth Stevens, New York, New York at 1-800-542-2595.

CONTENTS

Kinds of Sea Turtles.................................4

Keeping Count..6

Life of Danger...8

Human Use 10

Captured by Mistake 12

Pollution 14

Beachfront Property 16

Ocean Caretakers 18

Saving Sea Turtles 20

Glossary.. 22

For More Information 23

Index... 24

Words in the glossary appear in **bold** type the first time they are used in the text.

KINDS OF SEA TURTLES

Sea turtles live almost their whole lives in the ocean. Most live in warm ocean waters. There are seven **species** of sea turtles: olive ridley, Kemp's ridley, leatherback, green, hawksbill, loggerhead, and flatback.

The lives of all these sea turtles are filled with many dangers. These include **predators**, changes to **habitat**, hunters, fishing operations, and pollution. All species of sea turtles are endangered. This means there are so few left that they're at risk of dying out.

Some sea turtles can live in colder waters near Alaska, Canada, and Iceland. Most like warmer waters, though.

WILD FACTS
Like all **reptiles**, sea turtles breathe air.

5

KEEPING COUNT

The exact number of sea turtles isn't known. Male sea turtles spend their entire lives in the water, so it's impossible to count them. Instead, scientists **estimate** population numbers using the number of female sea turtles that come to shore to lay their eggs.

Female sea turtles swim thousands of miles to lay their eggs on sandy beaches. In most cases, they lay their eggs on the same beaches where they were born.

LIFE OF DANGER

Female sea turtles lay eggs in large groups called clutches, which they bury in the sand. There can be as many as 150 eggs in a clutch. A female may lay several clutches each year.

Predators—such as foxes, dogs, raccoons, birds, and crabs—often dig up the eggs and eat them. When the remaining eggs **hatch**, the baby turtles, or hatchlings, face a hard journey to the ocean. The same predators try to catch them as they crawl. Once in the ocean, hatchlings' predators include seabirds, crabs, and sharks.

WILD FACTS

The warmth of the sand decides whether an egg will become a male or female sea turtle.

For a sea turtle, the danger begins before it has even hatched.

9

HUMAN USE

People are the biggest **threat** to sea turtles. For hundreds of years, people hunted them and their eggs for food. Today, it's illegal to hunt sea turtles in many countries. However, illegal hunting, or poaching, still kills hundreds of thousands of sea turtles every year.

In addition to their meat, sea turtles are killed for their skin and shells. The skin of olive ridley turtles is used to make leather boots and shoes. People prize the shells of hawksbill turtles as well.

▼ Over 1 million olive ridley sea turtles were killed each year in Mexico during the 1960s.

11

CAPTURED BY MISTAKE

Sea turtles face threats from large fishing businesses. These operations use big nets to catch fish and shrimp, and sometimes sea turtles get caught in these nets. Sea turtles need to breathe air. They drown if the nets keep them from reaching the surface.

Long-line fishing operations use thousands of baited hooks to catch fish. Sea turtles can get caught on the hooks when they try to eat the bait. Even if a sea turtle escapes, it may be so badly hurt that it dies.

▼ Each year, hundreds of thousands of sea turtles are caught in fishing nets and on long-line hooks.

13

POLLUTION

Pollution in the ocean and on beaches is another threat to sea turtles. Plastic bags and other trash in the water can look like jellyfish, a favorite food for some sea turtles. If a sea turtle eats this trash, it can choke to death. Besides litter, wastewater, oil, and other spills can poison sea turtles and their habitats.

Litter on the beach is a problem for the smallest sea turtles. Hatchlings can get trapped in trash as they try to make their way to the ocean.

WILD FACTS

Some sea turtles, such as the green sea turtle, can live more than 80 years in the wild.

Some groups clean beaches regularly so that trash like plastic bags doesn't end up in the water.

BEACHFRONT PROPERTY

The number of people who live near coastlines is increasing. This has caused many problems for sea turtles and other sea animals. The construction of homes, businesses, and roads has changed and even taken away many beaches that sea turtles use for nesting. Boats can also harm or kill sea turtles.

Sea turtle hatchlings follow natural light shining on the water to find their way to the ocean at night. Lights from buildings **confuse** hatchlings and may cause them to head toward the buildings instead of the ocean.

WILD FACTS
As few as one in 1,000 sea turtle eggs produce turtles that live to be adults.

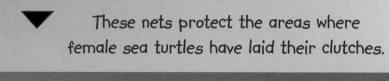

These nets protect the areas where female sea turtles have laid their clutches.

17

OCEAN CARETAKERS

Sea turtles are very important to the health of the ocean. Sea grasses on the ocean floor are home to many different **organisms**. Sea grasses need to be kept short in order to spread across the sea floor. Without sea turtles to eat the sea grasses, many organisms that live in the grasses could disappear.

Sea turtles also help keep beaches healthy. **Nutrients** from the eggshells of sea turtles help plants grow on beaches. Without those plants, the beach sands wash away.

WILD FACTS

Adult green sea turtles eat only sea grass and other ocean plants. All other sea turtles eat meat as well as plants.

Seaweed is important as a source of food and as a place for young turtles to hide.

SAVING SEA TURTLES

Many people understand how important sea turtles are to our world. Wildlife **conservation** groups are working with governments to protect sea turtles and their habitats. Some fishing nets now contain openings that allow trapped sea turtles to escape. People in coastal communities are told to turn off their lights during nesting season or to use special lights that won't confuse hatchlings.

In some areas, sea turtle populations are increasing. This means there's still hope for these animals. People can make a difference!

Estimated Populations of Nesting Female Sea Turtles

Kemp's ridley: 1,000

hawksbill: 8,000

flatback: 10,000

leatherback: 34,000

loggerhead: 60,000

green: 203,000

olive ridley: 800,000

GLOSSARY

confuse: to mix up

conservation: the care of the natural world

estimate: to make a guess based on knowledge or facts

habitat: an area where plants, animals, or other living things live

hatch: to come out of an egg

nutrient: something in food that helps a living thing stay healthy

organism: a living thing

predator: an animal that kills other animals for food

reptile: an animal that has scales, breathes air, and lays eggs. Turtles, snakes, crocodiles, and lizards are reptiles.

species: a group of animals that are all of the same kind

threat: something likely to cause harm

FOR MORE INFORMATION

BOOKS

Rhodes, Mary Jo, and David Hall. *Sea Turtles*. New York, NY: Children's Press, 2005.

Rodriguez, Cindy. *Sea Turtles*. Vero Beach, FL: Rourke Publishing, 2010.

Spilsbury, Louise. *Sea Turtle*. Chicago, IL: Heinemann Library, 2011.

WEBSITES

Marine Turtles
wwf.panda.org/what_we_do/endangered_species/marine_turtles/
Read all about sea turtles, and find out how you can help them.

Sea Turtles
www.nmfs.noaa.gov/pr/education/turtles.htm
Learn about six species of sea turtles.

Publisher's note to educators and parents: Our editors have carefully reviewed these websites to ensure that they are suitable for students. Many websites change frequently, however, and we cannot guarantee that a site's future contents will continue to meet our high standards of quality and educational value. Be advised that students should be closely supervised whenever they access the Internet.

INDEX

beaches 6, 14, 15, 16, 18

clutches 8, 17

eggs 6, 7, 8, 10, 16, 18

females 6, 7, 8, 17, 21

fishing 4, 12, 13, 20

flatback 4, 21

green 4, 14, 18, 21

habitat 4, 14, 20

hatchlings 8, 14, 16, 20

hawksbill 4, 10, 21

hooks 12, 13

hunters 4, 10

Kemp's ridley 4, 21

leatherback 4, 21

loggerhead 4, 21

males 6, 8

nesting 16, 20, 21

nets 12, 13, 17, 20

olive ridley 4, 10, 11, 21

people 10, 16, 20

plastic bags 14, 15

poaching 10

pollution 4, 14

predators 4, 8

sea grasses 18

species 4

threat 10, 12, 14

trash 14, 15